Speed Dating for Sperm Donors

Speed Dating for Sperm Donors

Natalie Meisner

Playwrights Canada Press
Toronto

For professional or amateur production rights, please contact:
The Playwrights Guild of Canada
350-401 Richmond St. West, Toronto, ON M5V 3A8
416.703.0201 :: info@playwrightsguild.ca

LIBRARY AND ARCHIVES CANADA CATALOGUING IN PUBLICATION
Title: Speed dating for sperm donors / Natalie Meisner.
Names: Meisner, Natalie D., 1972- author.
Description: First edition. | A play.
Identifiers: Canadiana (print) 20200189964 | Canadiana (ebook) 20200189972 | ISBN 9780369100825 (softcover) | ISBN 9780369100832 (PDF) | ISBN 9780369100849 (EPUB) | ISBN 9780369100856 (Kindle)
Classification: LCC PS8576.E433 S64 2020 | DDC C812/.54—dc23

Playwrights Canada Press operates on Mississaugas of the Credit, Wendat, Anishinaabe, Métis, and Haudenosaunee land. It always was and always will be Indigenous land.

We acknowledge the financial support of the Canada Council for the Arts—which last year invested $153 million to bring the arts to Canadians throughout the country—the Ontario Arts Council (OAC), Ontario Creates, and the Government of Canada for our publishing activities.

Canada Council for the Arts | Conseil des arts du Canada

ONTARIO ARTS COUNCIL
CONSEIL DES ARTS DE L'ONTARIO
an Ontario government agency
un organisme du gouvernement de l'Ontario

Canada

ONTARIO CREATES | ONTARIO CRÉATIF

For my wife and two sons,
who make every day a great adventure.

PREFACE

The beginning of the play you are about to read begins with the real-life story of my wife and I as we went about trying to make a family. It was important to her, as an adoptee and a woman of colour, to be able to provide knowledge of their lineage to any children we might create. In Canada most sperm bank donors are anonymous. Even those who indicate they can be contacted later still have an opt-out clause. So the seemingly smoothest route was closed to us. This was a deal breaker for her and we had to honour it.

This meant finding a known donor to be a member of our extended family. Not full-on co-parenting with financial or day-to-day duties, but we were offering a spot as one of those other important adults in our children's lives should we be successful. We also did not want to unnecessarily over-medicalize the process (you will see what this entails as you read on). This very intimate favour we were asking set us on a two-year journey of sit-downs with friends, friends of friends, other queer couples, and finally strangers that we contacted expressly for this purpose. My wife and I jokingly called this time "Speed Dating for Sperm Donors" and so now you know where I got the title. We had to cross so much unknown terrain with every new man we met, but also with the health system, legal documents, and socially about what we were trying to do. The world was not quite yet ready to welcome a family like ours.

We would tell stories of things that happened along with way to friends and they urged me to write about it. Indeed, when I looked into the literature there were a couple wonderful entries, but queer family making was certainly a field crying out for new work. I began making the notes for *Double Pregnant: Two Lesbians Make a Family* even as we were trying to get pregnant. As I did so, I took the oath of fidelity that I feel makes good non-fiction: to stick as close to the truth as I possibly could in that book. So no wincing away from the parts that hurt . . . but also no embellishing. Even if a situation was screaming out for me to crack my dramatic knuckles and give it a bit of mustard . . . I did not. At least not on purpose.

Enter stage left: Lunchbox Theatre's amazing Stage One Festival for new play development and the wonderful director and dramaturge, Pamela Halstead. We had a coffee sit-down on a wintery Calgary day in the downtown and I pitched an idea that had been brewing. What if I slightly fictionalized the characters from *Double Pregnant* (my wife and I!), thus allowing creative licence to really work with the comedy embedded in the situation. What if it were a big-hearted shaggy-dog biracial queer love story?

Pamela leaned forward. A happy ending story for families who don't fit the mould? Doesn't the world need more of that?

We decided it did.

As I described some of the scrapes my wife and I got into, and some of the real characters we met along the way, Pamela's brilliant laugh filled the coffee shop. That electric twinkle that so many of us in Canadian theatre will know by now told me we might have something.

And we were off. A successful debut as a one act at Lunchbox was soon followed by the full-length version in Halifax staged by DMV Theatre for Neptune Theatre, and then it was on to Ruby Slippers Theatre's Advance Theatre: New Works by Diverse Women in Vancouver.

We are so happy to bring it to you here in book form.

Natalie Meisner
Spring 2020

Speed Dating for Sperm Donors was developed as part of Lunchbox Theatre's Stage One Festival and was first produced as a one-act play by Lunchbox Theatre in Calgary on January 31, 2015, with the following cast and creative team:

Helen: Julie Orton
Paige: Janelle Cooper
Evan and others: Mark Bellamy
Trent, Tim, and others: Christian Goutsis

Director and Dramaturge: Pamela Halstead
Stage Manager: Megan Gurnsey
Assistant Stage Manager: Cale Thompson
Costume Design: Rebecca Toon
Sound Design: Dewi Wood
Set and Lighting Design: Dave Smith and Terry Gunvordahl

The play was later expanded into a full-length play produced by DMV Theatre and Neptune Theatre in Halifax on September 20, 2016, with the following cast and creative team:

Marty Burt
Kevin Curran
Micha Cromwell
Kathryn McCormack

Directed and Dramaturge: Pamela Halstead
Assistant Director: Emily Pettet
Stage Manager: Kate Redding
Apprentice Stage Manager: Robyn Gallant
Set Design: Garrett G. Barker
Lighting Design: Ingrid Risk
Costume Design: Jordyn Bochon
Sound Design: Ellis Lalonde

CHARACTERS

Helen: A teacher in her thirties from the east coast. She wants to have a baby with her partner, Paige.

Paige: A builder, also in her thirties, and a person of colour. She moved to Canada from France several years ago to be with Helen and also wants a baby.

Trent: Helen's best friend from her undergrad days. Worldly, a bit of a scamp, but big-hearted and hilarious. He comes from Calgary but has worked abroad for over a decade.

Tim and Evan: A couple who meet up with the women. Evan would like to be a donor for them. Tim . . . less so.

Waiter, Physicist, Lawyer, Hugger, Missionary Man, Louie, Kind Stranger, Various Men: A series of men who Helen and Paige go on "dates" with, in hopes that one of them will be a known sperm donor for them and help them start a family.

It is possible for all of the men's roles to be played by two actors.

SCENE I: FLAT OUT NO

PAIGE and HELEN's condo in Calgary, Alberta. There are signs of renovation underway. The kitchen space, however, is relatively intact and they sit having a drink with TRENT, HELEN's buddy from university.

TRENT drains his glass.

TRENT: That tasted like another.

(to HELEN) Grab you a cold one?

HELEN: No, I'm good.

He holds up HELEN's glass, sniffs.

TRENT: That's not even beer. What's in there?

HELEN: Just club soda—

TRENT: Club soda? That's not the Helen Murphy I knew in our tree-planting days.

PAIGE: Is that right?

TRENT: Drink me under the table, she could. Any man, woman, or beast in the tree-planting camp. Including the bush pilots.

HELEN: Now let's not exaggerate.

TRENT: Oh ho! Don't let this mild-mannered school-teacher persona she's rocking now fool you.

He jerks his thumb at HELEN.

Shotgun Helen they used to call her.

HELEN: Trent?

TRENT: Please don't tell me we've lost another one. You in recovery?

HELEN: No. I'm just . . . not drinking at the moment. Taking a break.

TRENT: A break. Alrighty then.

He offers a drink to PAIGE, *but she also shakes her head no.*

PAIGE: And for how much longer are you in town?

TRENT: Four days and counting, then it's back to the sandbox.

He glances at his watch.

Speaking of which, I got to take a whiz and then I should head. Going to the mountains early tomorrow to get my ski on.

He leaves for the washroom.

PAIGE: *Merde,* just ask him.

HELEN: I'm trying.

PAIGE: He's "the one" you say. Why hesitate?

HELEN: I'm working up to it.

PAIGE: If I must sit here drinking fizzy water until you pop the question, I'll explode.

HELEN: It's not that easy—

PAIGE: He leaves tomorrow. Back to Dubai.

HELEN: Doha.

PAIGE: Same thing.

HELEN: Actually, no—

PAIGE: They're both far. You know what I mean.

HELEN: I don't think I can do this. I better just write to him.

PAIGE: But you were waiting to ask him in person.

HELEN: True.

PAIGE: You are being such a girl right now.

HELEN: Being a girl—babe, I *am* a girl.

PAIGE: Do you want this or not?

HELEN: You know I do, but it's complicated. I think he might be seeing someone. He mentioned a woman's name when I was taking off his coat.

PAIGE: A woman?

HELEN: He's always hard to pin down with these things.

PAIGE: But he's supposed to be gay.

HELEN: *Supposed* to be?

PAIGE: We agreed to ask him because he's gay.

HELEN: We agreed to ask him 'cause he's my bestie—I never said he was gay.

PAIGE: But he has such great taste in clothes. His haircut, it's misleading.

HELEN: Women quite often think so, but no. Wait, are you saying he can't be our donor because he's straight? Because that would be reverse discrimination.

PAIGE: No—

HELEN: We'd be bigots backward. Backward bigots.

PAIGE: I just think that you could have warned me.

HELEN: How would that ever come up? Wait, that's not a deal breaker, is it? Just because he isn't?

TRENT has come back from the bathroom and overhears the very last bit.

TRENT: Isn't what?

They jump, surprised that he's back so quickly, and answer simultaneously:

HELEN: Aries. / **PAIGE:** Gay.

TRENT: Oh that.

HELEN: Paige!

TRENT: No worries, folks often assume—

PAIGE: Excuse me, I meant no—

TRENT: I'm not sure if it's my independent nature, or my pigheaded determination—

PAIGE: —offence.

TRENT: People quite often assume I am.

PAIGE: What?

TRENT: Aries.

PAIGE: Sorry?

HELEN: Oh, he's pulling your leg.

TRENT: Don't worry. I'm used to people thinking I'm gay after misspending my youth with this raging Sapphic whore.

HELEN claps a hand to her head in disbelief.

HELEN: Thanks.

TRENT is having fun teasing HELEN, but he isn't mean. He knows she can take a joke.

TRENT: *(to HELEN)* Don't mention it.

(to PAIGE) We both had our escapades, but she would jump any woman with short hair.

HELEN: Trent?

TRENT: Any woman wearing a plaid shirt. Any woman who looked sideways at her, really.

HELEN: Trent!

TRENT: Not that you could be picky in Cold Lake, Alberta. *Very* cold. Got to warm up somehow . . .

(to HELEN) Right, buddy?

HELEN: You're doing wonders for my home life here.

TRENT: Back in the day.

(to PAIGE) I mean—since you're all hitched up good and proper—I would assume that you've calmed her down a bit. Right?

Silence. PAIGE gives HELEN a look.

HELEN: This is going so well.

PAIGE: The thing is, Helen invited you over because she—I mean we—have something important to ask you.

TRENT: Is our evening about to take a turn for the weirder?

HELEN: Maybe we should just—

HELEN and PAIGE turn to one another, almost forgetting for a moment that they are not alone.

PAIGE: This is all you talk about and now here we have him right in front of us and—

PAIGE makes a gesture meaning "you do nothing."

Pfft.

HELEN: We're not asking to borrow his truck here . . . Gimme a minute.

TRENT: I hate to pry into your private business, but it seems you insist.

HELEN: Okay. Whew. We asked you over because we want a favour. A big favour. We . . . would like you to help us have a baby.

PAIGE: You don't need to do the intercourse.

HELEN: Paige!

PAIGE: That's what we agreed, no? Yes on the turkey baster, no on the penis.

TRENT: Now we know which side you come down on in that timeless debate.

HELEN takes a breath.

HELEN: Trent. My friend, my old friend and compatriot. Although it is always great to see you no matter what the circumstances . . . It's true we invited you here tonight with a bit of an agenda. We want to ask you to be the biological father of our child.

PAIGE: You won't have parental obligations. In fact, you don't need to be involved at all . . . after the first part.

HELEN: Unless you wanted to. I mean, if you wanted to be like an uncle or . . . that would be amazing, right?

PAIGE nods yes.

PAIGE: If you wanted, yes.

TRENT: Ah . . . I see.

HELEN: You pop by on a layover from New York to Bangkok. We'll have the baby washed and fed, cook you a meal—

PAIGE: If you do this for us. You will always be honoured in our house. He—or she—

TRENT gets up. He is shaking his head, but HELEN does not see him.

HELEN: Paige wants a boy, can you tell?

PAIGE: —will know who helped bring them into the world.

HELEN: This is perfect, Trent. All the fringe benefits of parenthood and none of the horrible green poop.

TRENT: *(quietly)* No, I . . .

HELEN: You regale us with stories of your life in the global trenches, we supply heartwarming anecdotes of family life. We'll live vicariously through one another over rounds of single malt . . .

PAIGE has noted his response, but HELEN has not.

PAIGE: *(gently)* Helen . . .

HELEN: The next morning we strap the baby in a car seat, grab lattes, I drop you at the airport—

TRENT: I said no.

HELEN: No?

TRENT: I can't do this . . . thing that you ask.

HELEN: But why not?

TRENT: This is such a huge—

HELEN: Not huge, tiny . . . We're just talking about one baby.

TRENT: I just can't.

HELEN: One tiny little baby with fingers and toes and . . .

TRENT: I'm sorry, sunshine.

TRENT gets up.

I hope you get what you want, but I'm . . . I'm not your guy.

HELEN: No?

He shakes his head no.

Oh.

TRENT: You're upset.

HELEN: No, I'm . . . not. I'm disappointed. Let's go with that. It has such a nice adult ring to it.

TRENT: While I'm not in a position to give you any essential bodily fluids . . . For what it's worth, I think you'd be great moms.

PAIGE: That's kind.

TRENT: Not to fret. You're resourceful ladies. If you want to get knocked up, I have no doubt in my mind that it is knocked up you will get.

He moves forward for a hug, but HELEN *doesn't respond. He kisses her quickly on the head. The two women wave as he leaves, holding hands for a moment. Blackout.*

SCENE 2: EUPHEMISMS WON'T HELP

HELEN *and* PAIGE *are in a dance club. Spots of light swirl around them. The music pulses for a moment and then softens.*

HELEN: My wife and I are out on the packed dance floor when she pops the question.

The music is pulsing—*oonch, oonch, oonch*—and the lasers splash light all over the wall, the floor, and us. Outside the snow just howls. It is the kind of storm that would bring things to a grinding halt anywhere else in the world, but here on the Canadian prairie . . . it only makes people commit to snow tires. Paige moved here from the south of France to be with me. The look on her face when she steps out into an Alberta clipper . . . is pretty much abject horror. And people don't help matters by telling her, "Oh, but it's a dry cold."

And so I've dragged my wife out dancing in the middle of a blizzard because I am afraid she's going to get cabin fever and then leave me.

I can barely hear her over the dance music when she asks:

The lights come on up PAIGE *for a moment.*

PAIGE: I said, do you want to have a baby with me?

HELEN: Holy shit! Did she just say what I think she just said? As a tomboy growing up in a fishing town in Nova Scotia, I never dared to dream that I would one day meet a woman from halfway around the world and fall in love. It seemed enough to hope for to get out unscathed. There was no such thing as gay marriage when I was young. There didn't seem to be any gay *people* for that matter. And so how could I imagine that I would one day walk hand in hand and carefree down the street with the woman I love? That I could ask her to marry me? How could I ever dare dream that she would be standing in front of me on the dance floor and asking me this?

A baby? Our own babies? To care for every day until they're grown?

Pause. HELEN *hugs herself, hands around both elbows.*

It's a question I never dared ask myself because it didn't seem possible. But, when she asks me, I have nothing to say but . . .

The lights come back up on PAIGE.

I do, I DO. Especially with you.

PAIGE: Wow. Okay, wow. Wow.

HELEN: Which one of us will carry the baby?

PAIGE: You! A baby from you would be so beautiful.

HELEN: Oh, I can just imagine a little Paige . . . you have to! Would you want a girl or a boy?

PAIGE: A boy. *Un petit garçon!* No . . . a little girl. Either! Both!

HELEN: Yes, you're right! We could do that. We could both have a baby!

PAIGE: They would be brothers—

HELEN: Or sister and brother.

PAIGE: Grow up together.

HELEN: They'd speak both languages.

PAIGE: Have two passports.

HELEN: The world will be their international oyster.

PAIGE: Like this we dream through one cold prairie winter.

HELEN: Thinking of sunny days in the park and sandcastles on the shoreline.

PAIGE: Our children's first steps. The books we'll read to them.

HELEN: We can imagine saying, in the not-too-distant future: "Finished your homework? Good. Now go get Mommy a beer so she can kick your ass at pool." Until it dawns on us that no amount of inspired conversation will get this done. If we really want to have a baby, we have to get down to brass tacks.

PAIGE: We must take action.

HELEN: Euphemisms won't help.

PAIGE: We are going to need sperm.

HELEN: Healthy, safe, fresh sperm.

PAIGE: And lots of it.

Lights fade.

SCENE 3: A FRIEND OF A FRIEND . . . OF A FRIEND

A funky tapas bar; a winter night. TIM *and* EVAN, *a couple, survey the menus and watch the door.*

EVAN: Oh, look, over there. That could be them.

TIM: I thought you said this was a friend.

EVAN: It is. A friend of a friend.

Pause. TIM *gives* EVAN *a look.*

Okay, of a friend.

TIM: Strangers? Tell me we are not on a blind date with a couple of strange lesbians.

TIM *shakes his fist in the air.*

Oh Fate, you are a fickle master.

EVAN: Maybe over there?

TIM: Pair of dykes . . . how hard can it be? Look for hefty girly men with matching plaid shirts.

EVAN: Be nice.

TIM: That *was* nice.

EVAN: Tim, Please?

Pause.

This is important to me. Imagine our child's first steps—

TIM: First time it throws up in your shoes—

EVAN: You get to see the whole world with fresh eyes.

TIM: —and hear it accompanied by the incessant droning whine of "mine, mine, mine!"

EVAN: Children take care of you in your twilight years.

TIM: You mean by infesting your house, spending all your money, and tossing you into an old folks' home at the end?

EVAN: Let's just hear these ladies out before we make any decisions.

TIM: I must love you.

EVAN: You do. It's just dinner. Try to be nice.

TIM: Now, pookie . . . when have I ever not been nice to strangers?

PAIGE and HELEN spot them and approach.

HELEN: Hi. Would you be Evan and . . . ?

EVAN: Yes. Please, come sit down.

HELEN: This is my wife, Paige. Really great of you to agree to meet up with us.

PAIGE: Hello.

EVAN: My husband, Tim.

PAIGE puts out her hand and shakes TIM's hand.

TIM: Firm handshake you've got there.

PAIGE: I am sorry. I worked with the mixer this morning.

TIM: Beg pardon?

HELEN: She's been making pilings for a shed. Mixing a little cement.

TIM: Mixing cement . . . delightful.

TIM shakes his head.

Lesbians!

An awkward pause that EVAN senses and breaks.

EVAN: So! Shall we order? This is one of our favourite little undiscovered gems. Excellent tapas . . .

HELEN: Yes, good idea.

PAIGE: The braised riblets, perhaps.

TIM holds up his hand.

TIM: Trust me, the ribs would be a disaster. I'll do the ordering.

PAIGE: But actually I do want the ribs—

HELEN has kicked her under the table.

Merde! What?

HELEN: So. Ah . . . maybe we should just let you know what kind of arrangement we have in mind.

EVAN: Yes, yes, do.

HELEN: When we started thinking about having children, we thought we could ask a close friend to be our donor. But that turned out to be complicated. For various reasons.

PAIGE: Her best friend said no.

EVAN: Really? I'm sorry to hear that.

HELEN: Thanks. It's okay—

PAIGE: We would like our children to know of their origins, to know who helped make them.

EVAN: I wouldn't mind. I'd like that.

PAIGE: No obligations, but to perhaps be someone special in their lives.

EVAN: I could do that. I could be special.

HELEN: To be clear, we are not asking you to take on parental responsibilities. All the day-to-day stuff, the financial obligations, caregiving . . . we have that covered.

PAIGE: Something like an uncle.

TIM: Uh oh . . . not a case of Uncle Daddy.

The women look at TIM.

EVAN: Don't mind him. It's his sense of humour, it's—

TIM: Acerbic?

EVAN: Endearing. In that it takes a while for you to warm up to it.

EVAN looks at the menu.

I think I'll have the miso-encrusted halibut bites.

TIM: You ordered them last time and they were greasy.

EVAN: You never let me order.

TIM: I do. Lord only knows how many greasy halibut bites I've choked down at your behest.

EVAN: Culinary martyrs of the world, we salute you.

TIM: Please don't let this be a repeat of Tampa.

PAIGE and HELEN get up, the men hardly noticing.

PAIGE: Excuse us—

PAIGE pulls HELEN after her.

We must go powder our noses.

HELEN: Powder our noses?

PAIGE: An English expression, no?

HELEN: Yes, circa 1958.

PAIGE: *On peut continuer en Française si tu préfère.*

HELEN: Okay—

PAIGE: *Vous avez deux langues officielles dans ce pays sacrément gelé, non? [You have two official languages in this damn frozen country, right?]*

HELEN: I get it. I'm sorry.

PAIGE: This guy, you know him from where?

HELEN: A friend of a friend.

PAIGE raises her eyebrows.

Of a friend.

PAIGE and HELEN eavesdrop for a moment. EVAN and TIM are arguing.

EVAN: I am ordering the halibut bites.

TIM: You ordered them last time and, not only were they greasy, they were limp.

EVAN: That won't be my only encounter with limpness this evening, I bet.

HELEN: Why are they fighting? Wouldn't you think they'd try to make a good impression?

PAIGE: What if they *are* trying?

Beat. That is a scary thought.

HELEN: Maybe they're just nervous. Come on.

PAIGE: I follow you.

HELEN: That's my girl.

They come back in.

EVAN sees them, jumps up, and pulls out their chairs. They are unused to chivalry, and EVAN is unaccustomed to delivering it. There is some awkwardness and stepping on toes before they settle.

EVAN: You're back. Please sit down. Why don't you tell us all about how you envision this process?

HELEN: Okay, sure. Well, the whole ovulation thing is tricky. It doesn't come the same time every month. You have to do a test that detects a surge in hormone levels.

PAIGE: You pee on a stick.

TIM: Do you? Pee on a stick . . . Fascinating.

HELEN: The window of opportunity is quite small. Forty-eight hours, but the first twenty-four are really the best. So, when we get the positive sign, we'll need to have you on speed dial.

EVAN: Definitely. Now where would I make the ah . . . I mean, would you prefer that I . . .

TIM: Are you blushing? I can't say I remember the last time you blushed about *anything*, let alone the . . . what shall we call it in this context? Baby batter?

HELEN: Wherever you feel most comfortable. Your place, if you like, and then come over to ours.

PAIGE: You must keep it warm. Sperm die if they get cold. You put it next to your skin so it takes your body heat.

TIM: I think I'll have the prawns. They come in a cream sauce.

Pause. Everyone decides to carry on.

PAIGE: We have a donor agreement that you can read.

HELEN: Yes. To be clear, we aren't looking to co-parent. What would be best, we think, is someone who would enjoy having a child in their life occasionally.

TIM: I hate to say I told you so, but hear that? Not a real daddy.

EVAN: Tim, please!

TIM: I'm the daddy in this relationship. Let's go home and I'll turn you over my knee . . . you'll forget this ever happened.

HELEN: Do you mind not doing that?

TIM: Beg pardon?

HELEN: Sexualizing a parental term—

TIM: Oh snap, Gloria Steinem. I happen to be an out and proud bear using the term daddy in reference to a mutually agreed upon S/M scenario. And the last time I checked, no one owned language.

HELEN: Of course, it's just that in this context it's a bit . . .

HELEN turns to PAIGE for support.

Paige?

PAIGE: He has a point, Helen.

TIM turns to the women.

TIM: But hold on, ladies—though I use *that* term as loosely as a Catholic schoolgirl on spring break—we haven't *agreed* to any of this.

EVAN: Tim, we're just discussing the possibility—

HELEN: Right. This is just a first meeting. We aren't assuming—

PAIGE looks at TIM.

PAIGE: Unless I am wrong, you are not the one who would be the donor.

TIM: No. But that *(indicates EVAN)* is my man. That *(indicates area)* is my man's junk, and I have a say over where it goes and what he does with it.

HELEN: Do you even like children?

TIM: Children are delicious.

EVAN: He means in an abstract way.

TIM: I mean in "A Modest Proposal" way: pan-seared with saffron and a side of microgreens.

Both women react and so does EVAN. The women may push back from the table. EVAN may try and do damage control and keep them seated. The next lines all come simultaneously in response:

HELEN: Okay, that's just— **PAIGE:** *N'est pas drôle.* **EVAN:** Tim!

PAIGE: This will not work.

(to EVAN) It seems you want to be a full-time papa.

(to TIM) And you—

EVAN: No, no. Uncle would be okay.

TIM: Liar.

EVAN: Why are you ruining this for me?

TIM: Excuse me, darling, if I don't leap at the chance to buckle myself into the minivan of conformity with a couple of baby-crazed lesbians and go hurtling down the superhighway of mediocrity.

TIM tosses his napkin into his plate and storms off to the washroom. They all watch him go for a moment and then:

PAIGE: So, do you, ah . . . you go after him, or . . .

EVAN: No, no. Best not to react when he acts out like that.

A WAITER with a thick Australian accent approaches the table. He steps in front of EVAN.

WAITER: Excuse you, mate. Couldn't help but overhear . . . I'd be happy to help you Sheilas out.

They think he means with food or ordering, but no, he continues.

My grandfather lived to be 101. Never sick a day in his life. I have a break in ten minutes . . .

EVAN: I don't believe this.

WAITER: *(lower)* Of course, it would be great if you were able to reflect that level of customer service in the tip.

EVAN: Beat it.

WAITER: You got it.

HELEN and PAIGE again push back from the table. EVAN doesn't have it in him to try and stop them.

PAIGE: We thank you, anyway, for your time . . .

EVAN: You're leaving? But we haven't even ordered . . .

HELEN: *(to EVAN)* I have your contact info. Maybe we could go for coffee sometime?

EVAN: Yes, let's.

PAIGE: *(under her breath)* Maybe, as you say, "plan B." We get the waiter's number?

Lights fade as they exit.

SCENE 4: STRANGERLAND

PAIGE and HELEN are in their favourite coffee shop in Calgary with their computers and newspapers.

HELEN: This is harder than I thought.

PAIGE: We've been here in Calgary such a short time. Who can we ask for this kind of favour?

HELEN: Can we find a way to put everything on pause? Go to France?

PAIGE: Impossible to leave work. For a couple weeks, maybe, but it's not long enough.

HELEN: We could bring someone over here. What about your brother?

PAIGE: My brother?

HELEN: He's so great! Not to mention handsome . . . and since you aren't biologically related—

PAIGE: True, we are not blood, but he's my brother still.

HELEN: He could be a donor for me and we find someone else for you.

PAIGE: But they won't be related to one another.

HELEN: We might have to make compromises if we really want this to happen.

PAIGE: Perhaps, but not my brother. Feels too strange. What about your relations?

HELEN: Tons of girl cousins. And a few guys, too, but they are all in the busiest part of raising their own kids. What about that friend of yours who wants to come for a visit?

PAIGE: Andre? Sure, I'll ask him to plan his ski trip based on our fertility cycles.

HELEN: I know, right?

PAIGE: And if he says no? After what happened with your friend . . .

HELEN: There is that.

PAIGE: Have you talked to him? Maybe time to call?

HELEN: I should. I will. Maybe it should be someone we know less well. Or even someone we don't know at all.

HELEN slides a pamphlet over to PAIGE.

PAIGE: A catalogue?

PAIGE reads.

A sperm donor catalogue. You know how I feel about this.

HELEN: I know, but they give you their profiles, so we'll know some things about them.

PAIGE: Height, weight, eye colour? Tells you nothing.

HELEN: You can also see where the donor comes from. Look, here's a guy from Cameroon.

PAIGE: And so? Do you know, Helen, that the clinics freeze the sperm? It is less effective. And just feels . . . wrong.

HELEN: What do you mean, wrong? Why?

PAIGE: I don't know . . . cold. To begin a life this way . . . I understand that it can be okay for some. But not for me.

PAIGE turns away. She puts her arms around her own shoulders as if she also feels the chill. HELEN approaches her and warms her up.

I am sorry. It is a feeling and I can't explain it . . .

HELEN: Okay. I understand. Then what are we going to do?

PAIGE: There must be someone.

(suddenly) Ask Syd.

HELEN: My squash partner? No way.

PAIGE: *Pourquoi pas?*

HELEN: Can you have an in-depth conversation with a two-inch piece of rubber whizzing past your head? You work with guys all day. You ask someone. That granite guy. Who does the countertops. He's nice. And cute too.

PAIGE: Kyle? He's a stranger, nearly.

HELEN: And if he said no you wouldn't lose your best friend. Maybe that's exactly what we need.

PAIGE: At work? I don't think I can. There must be other women doing what we are doing. Try to look it up.

HELEN: Look it up? What, like google it?

PAIGE: Why not?

HELEN flips her computer open and types in a search term.

HELEN: Okay. Looking for . . .

Tap, tap.

Sperm . . .

Tap.

Nasty things start popping up and she tries to click them away, aware that they are in a café.

No. Ew!

Click, click.

Go away.

Click, click.

That's so wrong.

PAIGE: What is it?

HELEN: Just playing whack-a-mole with porn sites here.

PAIGE looks at the screen, laughs. HELEN continues clicking away images. When one of the sites initiates audio, she closes the lid, shutting it down.

PAIGE: Maybe different search terms. Try "sperm donors."

HELEN: Okay. If my hard drive isn't fried already.

HELEN peeks under the lid and starts searching again.

Here's something. *D-I-Y Baby.*

PAIGE: Do it yourself . . . *j'aime ça.*

HELEN: No donors, though. This is more like a set of instructions.

PAIGE: That's useful. We save it for later. Look, here: Co-parents dot com.

HELEN: There's a minefield. All the decisions about schools, health, food, rules. Hard enough to do as a couple. Can you imagine doing it by committee with people you don't even know?

PAIGE: People look for all sorts of arrangements. Some co-parents . . . mild involvement . . . and involvement after the age of eighteen.

HELEN: Here's another site: *Global Sperm Donors.* Donors and people seeking donors can find each other. Look, you can browse by country. Even province.

PAIGE slides over, reads.

PAIGE: Anyone near us?

HELEN: Here's a lesbian couple. Looking for a donor. A straight couple . . . looking. Another couple need a surrogate. A single woman . . .

PAIGE reads.

PAIGE: Two more lesbians . . . They want to form a support group.

HELEN: Trust lesbians to form a support group right out of the gate. There'll be a potluck, no doubt.

PAIGE: Why can't I find profiles of the men?

HELEN: Here's something I thought I'd never see.

PAIGE: What?

HELEN: Paige cruising for guys on the Internet.

PAIGE: Enough from you now. Here's one . . . Delbert from Edmonton.

HELEN: Roads are starting to clear. I'd drive to Edmonton for fresh sperm.

PAIGE: Healthy, STI-free . . .

HELEN: Good, good.

PAIGE: Twenty-two years old.

HELEN: Oh.

HELEN moves to read over her shoulder.

"Will drive to your house and take as much time to get as many women pregnant as needed." As many women as needed? How many does he think we have over here?

PAIGE: Very generous with his time.

HELEN: Here's one. Ex-CFL linebacker. Based in San Diego but comes to town for business.

PAIGE: His username: DaHulk? Like the Incredible Hulk. We can have little green babies.

HELEN: Says he's a card-carrying member of Mensa.

PAIGE: Very intelligent little green babies, ripping out of their onesies. Lifting us up over their heads. "You won't like baby when he's angry!"

HELEN returns to the site.

HELEN: Says he's an investor in oceanfront land. Owns several yachts. Works with Doctors Without Borders . . . and is also the advisor to several heads of state.

PAIGE: Hm. Too good to be true?

HELEN: A fourteen-year-old with an overactive imagination.

PAIGE: Maybe we should make a profile.

HELEN: Put ourselves out there . . . on the interwebs, in strangerland, for anyone to contact?

PAIGE: You write it for us.

HELEN: Yeah? What do I write?

PAIGE: Say who we are . . . what we like to do.

HELEN starts writing.

HELEN: Hi. We're Paige and Helen. We like travelling and cooking . . .

She stops.

"And long walks on the beach." Sounds like dating.

PAIGE: It is, I suppose. Only different. Keep going.

HELEN: So we are . . . doing this? Right now?

PAIGE: *Oui.*

HELEN: Okay, here we need to check a box for AI or NI. What does that mean? Artificial Insemination. And NI . . . Natural Insemination. Natural? That means that people are actually . . .

PAIGE: With strangers. No. Oh no. Mark AI. This box for certain.

A pause. They are quiet.

We'll get this done, right?

HELEN: Yes, girl. We already crossed continents, uprooted our lives to be together.

PAIGE: We love each other.

HELEN: That we do.

PAIGE: It will happen. I'm not sure how yet, but it will.

Lights fade.

SCENE 5: SMASH IT NOW

PAIGE is renovating the condo. She has a mallet in her hand and is considering a wall in the kitchen.

PAIGE: If I take this wall down, we have space enough for a nursery.

PAIGE gestures.

It is load bearing, so a beam must be placed to do the job of the wall. But the question is . . . do I take it down now or wait?

I hope to be a good mama. I know I have things to show a child: how to build things, how to solve problems . . . how to be kind. But a tiny infant? So small, so helpless. I won't know how to hold him or what to do if he cries.

Pause. She takes measurements with a tape.

I was three when my maman and papa—they were so happy—brought me home from the orphanage. It was a crowded one. Not enough arms to pick up the babies, so I wasn't used to being held. They got me used to it, slowly.

In the photo albums, I suddenly appear: one dark face among the lighter ones. No records of where I came from. They thought, then, that it was better for a child not to know.

She shakes her head.

I fit in well but there was this slight . . . hesitation when I was called by my new name. The same hesitation of the mothers when they saw me on the playground: "To whom does this one belong, then?" To talk about this . . . is difficult in English. Even back before the French, there is another tongue . . . that I remember only as bright sounds and colours.

Beat.

But you must not hear this as complaint. I was wanted. I was loved. My parents made the best nest for me. But the woman who carried me, the man who fathered me—I never stop wondering . . . do they walk this earth? Do they breathe, still? What could happen so terrible that you abandon the child to whom you gave life?

She pauses, takes out a handkerchief, and wipes her forehead.

And so, if we have children, they will know who made them. And I will be there, constant and strong from the very first moment. Because even animals—wild animals—will kill creatures several times their own size before leaving their babies. Anything else is . . .

Excuse me. I was very small. Remembering it makes me feel things that I do not understand.

She turns back to the wall.

I can see it now: this will work for a nursery.

What do you think? Smash it now, or wait?

I think: take it down now and hope for the best.

Smash, bang, crash as she crunches into the drywall with the mallet.

SCENE 6: TOTAL WORLD DOMINATION

A brisk spring day. HELEN *and* PAIGE *stand outside near the arrivals gate at the airport. They blow into their hands and stamp their feet. The whoosh of airplanes can be heard.*

PAIGE: Why is it we must meet him at the airport?

HELEN: He's on a tight schedule, I guess. He gave very specific instructions. I wasn't about to question them.

PAIGE: Is he coming home with us, or—

HELEN: I'm not sure. There he is.

A man in a Russian fur hat enters.

PHYSICIST: You are on time. This is most excellent.

HELEN: Thank you so much for agreeing to meet us.

PAIGE: Can we, perhaps, go and sit down together—

PHYSICIST: No, this location is serviceable.

HELEN: Okay, well why don't you tell us a little about yourself?

PHYSICIST: Here, I have photograph. Myself as little baby. You may keep.

HELEN *and* PAIGE *lean over the picture.*

HELEN: Awww. Very cute.

PAIGE: This must be your maman holding you?

PHYSICIST: No. This is wet nurse in Mother Russia Young Physicist Training Facility.

HELEN: Yes, you mentioned you were a physicist in your message. Maybe you could tell us about your work.

PHYSICIST: Black hole physics, yes. I make superconductor simulations embedded in flat space. I propose new type of ultralight particle forming halos supported by the quantum uncertainty principle.

HELEN: Wow. That sounds . . . Wow.

HELEN elbows PAIGE.

Paige?

PAIGE: Impressive. Very impressive.

PHYSICIST: Quite standard, actually, compared to former research. But we dispense now with pleasantries. I go to produce required material. You will kindly have transcripts ready for my return.

HELEN: Transcripts?

PHYSICIST: You both completed university training, yes? My requirement for distribution of genetic material is that you score in top ninety-five percentile. Equivalent of your North American A+. I am not wanting to mix my genetics with inferior specimens. Kindly produce documents to prove your intelligence level.

HELEN: We don't have any documents with us.

PHYSICIST: Most inconvenient. My flight departs at two P.M. Ah.

He whips out a notepad and sketches.

I now pose you theorem of moderate difficulty. You have solution by the time I have sample . . . no problem.

He hands the theorem over to them and leaves.

HELEN: He didn't say anything about a test!

PAIGE: What does that mean, "inferior specimens"? Is he going behind a pillar?

HELEN: Could it be a language problem?

PAIGE cranes her neck.

PAIGE: I think it's a bigger problem—he's a crackpot!

HELEN: Very smart people, I have noticed, are often quite odd. Let's just ask him some more questions. Meantime . . . here, you better do this.

She slides the notepad paper over to PAIGE.

PAIGE: No, you.

HELEN: I'm not touching it. You're math girl.

PAIGE: Normal math, not black hole physics!

HELEN: Try. Write *some*thing!

They throw it back and forth. The PHYSICIST returns and PAIGE quickly writes down an answer.

We just wanted to ask you: Why do you want to be a donor?

PHYSICIST: It is most efficient. Statistically speaking, I would never have time to personally impregnate all of the women who now have borne me children.

PAIGE: All of the women? How many are there?

PHYSICIST: Two hundred and thirty-nine this year.

HELEN: This year alone?

PHYSICIST: Total number of known progeny since I begin experiment is two thousand seven hundred and twenty-one.

He reaches inside his jacket pocket, and HELEN *and* PAIGE *both take a step back.*

But we waste time. Sample is getting cold.

PAIGE: Why do you do this?

PHYSICIST: Covert distribution of superior genetic footprint. End result: total world domination. But don't worry about that. Very cute babies. Look at photograph.

PAIGE: I don't think we can be a part of your experiment.

He is examining the theorem on the notepad.

PHYSICIST: Unfortunately, you are correct. Three? The answer you propose to theorem is three?

PAIGE: *Oui?*

He does a little bow.

PHYSICIST: It is my disappointing duty to inform you that you are not viable subjects. I now proceed to Cincinnati to next potential vessel. Goodbye.

He gives another little bow and makes an abrupt departure.

HELEN: Nice to meet you too.

Lights fade.

SCENE 7: THE FINE PRINT

PAIGE and HELEN wait for their next date at a coffeeshop. They already have their coffees in to-go cups.

HELEN spots him.

HELEN: This one's a lawyer. Navy blue jacket, three o'clock.

She waves.

Ready?

PAIGE: All right. Let's do this.

HELEN: Here he comes.

The LAWYER enters with a briefcase. He surveys the women quickly then places his briefcase on the table between them with a thud.

LAWYER: Good day.

PAIGE: Nice to meet you. I'm Paige and—

She extends a hand for a shake. He gestures "one moment" as he flips open the briefcase.

LAWYER: One moment. Before we go any further, I'll need you to sign this, authorizing me to make a recording and transcript of today's conversation.

PAIGE: Is it necessary? I mean, we are only beginning to talk—

He shakes his head; they don't get it.

LAWYER: Anyone familiar with the conflicted state of Canadian donor law would agree.

HELEN: Okay . . . I guess.

They sign, somewhat reluctantly.

LAWYER: Surely you wouldn't expect anyone to engage haphazardly in assisted reproduction without protecting himself.

HELEN: We brought a standard contract for sperm donors. It releases you from all financial obligation.

LAWYER: When you've been practising law for as long as I have, you come to understand that the terms "standard" and "contract" are mutually exclusive.

HELEN: It's the Canadian version. We downloaded it from the Internet.

That is a knee-slapper.

LAWYER: Oh-ho ho! The Internet!

He sets up his recorder.

All right. I'll need you on record with regards to your stance on Lavine versus British Columbia.

HELEN: We have done some research but aren't familiar with that case in particular.

LAWYER: Stratten v. Billingsly?

HELEN: No, ah . . .

LAWYER: The AHRA of 2004?

HELEN's hand shoots up involuntarily.

HELEN: I know that one! Bill C-6. Assisted Human Reproduction Act.

PAIGE: Don't you think we should get to know one another a bit first?

HELEN: Yes, why don't you tell us why you want to be a donor?

LAWYER: Are you familiar with the concept of opportunity cost?

He looks up. They are shaking their heads no, so he continues.

Measures the cost of any activity in terms of the next best alternative. I am fifty and single. I haven't had a date in over two years, so at this point I'm unlikely to have children in the normal way.

PAIGE: By "normal," you mean what?

PAIGE begins to rankle. HELEN puts a hand on her arm to calm her.

HELEN: Paige.

(to LAWYER) It's certainly not too late to fall in love.

LAWYER: I have pretty much given up on that as well.

HELEN: Oh. That's kind of . . . sad.

LAWYER: Perhaps.

Beat.

But emotions are of no help in contractual negotiations.

PAIGE: *(to HELEN)* Is he trying to make a joke?

HELEN: I think what Paige is saying is we'd like to get to know you a bit first.

The LAWYER sighs.

LAWYER: I was raised in Red Deer in a household of moderate income. My hobbies include archery, model building, and swimming.

PAIGE: So you're a swimmer . . .

LAWYER: Upon entering a body of water I do not, immediately, sink. Do you wish to proceed?

He looks up and they nod, a bit taken aback. He continues.

While article 12.6 of the Children's Law Act clearly states that "a man whose semen is used to artificially inseminate a woman to whom he is not married or with whom he is not cohabiting at the time is not, in law, the father of the resulting child—"

HELEN: There, that seems to clear it up, then—

LAWYER: Not so. There is precedent in the US—McGrath v. the State of Kansas. McGrath agreed to donate sperm to two women, acquaintances of his. Your "standard" agreement was used. The three lose touch until ten years later when he receives a *summons.* It seems the women fell on hard times and applied for government housing. The responsibility to provide for the child he helped create passed from these two insolvent women to the unsuspecting McGrath.

PAIGE: We are not insolvent. And we would never ask a donor for child support.

LAWYER: You're not listening. The women themselves did not launch the suit. The State of Kansas did. This one is ongoing, so you'll want to watch it closely.

HELEN: So what you are saying is that there is no way to really protect the donor—or us, for that matter.

He leans forward, turns off the recording.

LAWYER: Everything's negotiable, I'm afraid. That's why they pay us the big bucks. Shall we continue?

They nod yes. He turns the recording back on.

PAIGE: Is here any document that would make you comfortable?

LAWYER: Here we are. In triplicate.

He drops a fat stack of documents on the table.

I think you'll find this superior to the one you found on "the Internet."

HELEN takes the document and begins to read it. It is long. Meanwhile, the LAWYER continues.

As with any type of third-party contract, the law governing the rights and obligations of known sperm donors is complex. And varies significantly among jurisdictions, indeed even sometimes within a given jurisdiction.

HELEN continues to read the document as he speaks.

The legal parentage provisions in British Columbia's new Family Law Act, for example, deal specifically with parentage in situations of assisted conception defined as "a method of conceiving a child other than by sexual intercourse—"

HELEN points to a part of the document.

HELEN: What does this mean, right here? *Volenti non fit injuria.*

LAWYER: Injury cannot be done to the willing. Just another way of saying that you know what you are signing.

HELEN: I see. And this? *Vinculum Juris.*

LAWYER: Chains of the law, literally. Just means legally binding.

HELEN: I mean, my Latin is a little rusty, but clause fifty-eight subsection B seems to state that if we died, you would inherit all of our assets?!

PAIGE grabs HELEN's hand and pulls her up.

PAIGE: Veto. That's the only Latin I know.

HELEN: Ditto. What she said, veto.

They exit.

SCENE 8: THE SACRED HERB OF WOMEN

An outdoor park. HELEN *and* PAIGE *look for their next date.*

HELEN: I really hope this one isn't a hugger.

PAIGE: Yes, you Canadians, always hugging. Arms go this way and that way. It's very awkward. Why not a simple kiss on the cheek?

HELEN: That's not simple. First of all, how do you know which cheek to go for first?

PAIGE *waves her hand.*

PAIGE: Left, always.

HELEN: And then do you actually kiss them, or just touch your cheek to theirs? I put the lips to that aunt of yours in Corsica and she was not impressed.

PAIGE: *Tante* Pauline offers the cheek to everyone. That's just her way.

HELEN: And then there's not even a set number of kisses.

PAIGE *shrugs.*

PAIGE: You feel it out as you go.

HELEN *glances at her watch.*

HELEN: Do you want to handle background info or the logistics this time?

PAIGE: Logistics.

HELEN: It feels like we are getting really good at this routine.

PAIGE: I don't want to get any better.

HELEN: Do you think we should tell him we're seeing other guys?

PAIGE: Not unless he asks.

HELEN: But isn't that like cheating, in a way? What if we get a reputation for being "players"—

PAIGE: In the lesbians seeking men for baby-making subculture?

HELEN: Could happen.

PAIGE: Take a deep breath now and tell me: What do we know?

HELEN flips open a notepad and reads out the highlights.

HELEN: Early thirties, a dancer. Open to casual contact afterward . . . oh, it says he volunteers with Guerilla Gardeners. That's pretty cool. You know, that organization downtown that takes vacant lots and plants food that anyone can eat.

HELEN spots him approaching.

Okay, here we go.

A man approaches. He is wearing long, unbleached cotton pants and a vest. He carries two bundles of branches tied up with coloured string.

HUGGER: Paige. Helen.

HELEN: No, I'm Helen and—

HUGGER: Helen. Paige.

He immediately seizes PAIGE *in a hug. She tries to return it but begins to stiffen.*

HELEN: Hi. Okay. So, we thought maybe we'd walk through the park and then maybe stop somewhere and grab a coffee?

HUGGER: No, I don't partake of caffeine. It violently recalibrates the metabolism.

HELEN: Or a soda or juice—

HUGGER: I require nothing at the moment.

HELEN: Okay, well, let's all get acquainted. I think I mentioned to you that I'm a teacher—

He holds up his hand for silence and peers meaningfully into their eyes.

HUGGER: I have brought you a gift. I spent the morning gathering this for you in the ravine.

He presents them with the bundles of braches. The women take them reluctantly.

It is sage. Sage promotes fertility and is also the sacred herb of women.

HELEN: Oh, that's . . . sacred herb of women. Huh, didn't know that—did you know that, Paige?

PAIGE: No. Nope. I didn't.

Pause.

So shall we begin by speaking a little about the arrangement we have in mind?

HUGGER: I would love that, but can we first mark the beginning of our knowing of one another with a moment?

He peers first into HELEN's eyes . . . then PAIGE's. He says nothing but seems to find the silence full and satisfying. The women . . . not so much. They try to pull away from his gaze, but he holds it. He means a full moment.

HELEN: So nice of you—

HUGGER: Shh. I am reading your aura right now.

HELEN: *(whispering)* What does it say?

HUGGER: I'm seeing a stipple of greys and light purple with pink undertones.

HELEN: Is that a good thing?

HUGGER: This tells me you are giver. Always taking care of the people in your life.

The HUGGER turns to PAIGE.

You have a very forceful energy. You like to work with your hands. I think we have a strong connection. Can you feel that, flowing between us right now?

PAIGE: I feel something flowing, yes. Helen says you are a dancer. What kind of dance do you do?

HUGGER: You probably wouldn't know it.

PAIGE: Oh? What is it? Salsa dancing? Tango? Modern dance?

HUGGER: I am a contact improvisation artist. It is a form without preconceived steps or patterns.

PAIGE: What kind of music do you dance to?

HUGGER: Actually, it's done without music.

PAIGE: Do you have a partner that you dance with often?

HUGGER: Contact improvisation is typically done in pairs. But I do solo work.

PAIGE: So, no steps, no music, and no partner?

HUGGER: Lately most of my work has been partnering with the floor.

PAIGE: Sorry, can you say that again? I must have misunderstood. I thought you said your partner was the floor.

HUGGER: No. I said I partner *with* the floor. And sometimes the wall.

HELEN: Do you have any performances coming up?

HUGGER: It is not about the performance.

HELEN: That sounds great. So, I think I mentioned that Paige works in restoration.

HUGGER: Fascinating. What do you restore?

PAIGE: Houses.

HELEN: When we met, she was working on a castle in France.

PAIGE: Not a castle. A typical house for the region.

HELEN: Five storeys, stone walls, and Knights Templar crests. A castle by Canadian standards. And she's also working on a fisherman's cottage in Nova Scotia.

HUGGER: Do you live in all of these places?

PAIGE: For a time. And sell them after. Except for our place by the sea. It is work for me. Though I love it, too.

HUGGER: You have to do what you love. I was in banking. I was so unhappy.

Pause.

Then one morning . . . this strong message came—directly from my body. My body simply refused to be stuffed into that three-piece jailhouse called a suit. And ever since I followed that message . . . my life has done a complete one-eighty. I have found true friendship. I have come to know the meaning of community.

HELEN: Yes, in your message you mentioned the community garden. That's great. If we—when we have children—we really want to teach them those kinds of values.

PAIGE: We are looking for a donor, not a co-parent.

HUGGER: That's good. I don't see myself in any kind of heavy authoritarian role.

PAIGE: Someone who would be known to the child as his biological father.

HUGGER: I am completely open to that. Now you told me your vision of the future, would it be all right if I tell you mine? Then we could see if there are natural points of convergence between them.

HELEN: Sure, that would be great.

HUGGER: After we combine our essences and produce another life, I would like to remain close to you. Very close.

The HUGGER turns to PAIGE.

Your aura is looking very speckly right now.

His phone rings. The ring tone is the opening of "Orinoco Flow."

Sorry. Please excuse me for one moment, I have to take this . . .

He steps aside.

PAIGE: My aura wants to go home.

HELEN: I know, sweetie.

PAIGE picks up the sage.

PAIGE: The sacred herb of women?

HELEN: Well I didn't know that, did you? Listen, he means well.

PAIGE: I just can't imagine . . . making a child with him.

HELEN: Look, we'll wrap it up, go home, and talk about all of the options together, all right?

He is on the phone, at a distance. He smiles to them, "I'll be right there."

PAIGE: Okay.

SCENE 9: MAGIC ELIXIR

PAIGE and HELEN are in their condo. Home improvements continue and there are even more construction materials.

HELEN: I can't believe this. I can't believe we are actually going to do this.

PAIGE: I am going to make you pregnant. Are you nervous?

HELEN: Excited. So kind of him to come over to our place.

PAIGE: Yes. How long do you think it takes?

HELEN: No idea. It varies, I suppose . . .

Pause.

PAIGE: It's too quiet.

HELEN: Maybe we should turn on some music?

PAIGE: What do we listen to for this occasion?

HELEN: Whew. I don't know.

PAIGE scrolls through songs on computer and finds something quite unsuitable, like Bette Midler singing "Wind Beneath My Wings."

PAIGE: Not that. This?

She plays a sexy song. Something like Barry White's "Can't Get Enough of Your Love, Babe."

HELEN: No! Not sexy music.

PAIGE tries another that just does not work, like Lesley Gore's "It's My Party."

PAIGE: Definitely not that. Turn on the television?

HELEN: What if something horrible comes on in the exact moment that our baby—

PAIGE: Not a baby yet.

HELEN: Okay . . . the beginning of our maybe-baby is . . . happening.

It is quiet—too quiet. They pace around the room.

PAIGE: Did you leave him the . . . reading material?

HELEN: Yes, a whole stack. I got into the store and just realized that I had no idea what to get. I mean, how do we ever know what it is on this earth that appeals to another person—so I grabbed the whole rack and threw them in my basket.

PAIGE: All of them? You naughty girl.

HELEN: I didn't want the lady at the corner shop thinking I was a sex maniac, so I threw some gum and three packages of cheese on top . . . for camouflage.

PAIGE: So . . . a sex maniac who really loves cheese.

HELEN: Stop.

PAIGE: Seems right to me—

HELEN: Shh . . . Did you hear that? Is he coming?

PAIGE: Maybe better not to say "coming." In French it's even worse: *j'arrive*—

HELEN: Stop it! I don't want to be . . . giggling.

PAIGE: Why not?

HELEN: While he's upstairs making the—

PAIGE: Magic elixir? What did the other guy say? Baby batter.

HELEN: Please.

They hear a noise. Water running upstairs.

PAIGE: That's him.

HELEN: He knows we have to put it in right away, right?

PAIGE: Yes, I told him.

HELEN: So he's not going to hang around.

PAIGE: Yes, relax.

HELEN: You go and . . . get it from him.

PAIGE: Why me?

HELEN: Because I'm the one being impregnated. Makes sense for you to handle it.

PAIGE: You can't just make up new rules as you like.

HELEN: Please?

PAIGE: Okay.

She smooths her hands over her face and turns. The HUGGER *enters with a small pill bottle.*

HUGGER: Paige. Helen.

He moves forward for a hug, then remembers and stops himself.

I leave you to it. Sending vibrations of fecundity from over here.

PAIGE *grabs him and pulls him in for a quick hug.*

PAIGE: Thank you.

HELEN: Yes, thank you so much!

PAIGE: We will let you know if we have been successful as soon as we know.

HUGGER: I hold you in my thoughts as you embark on this great adventure. Namaste.

He puts his shoes on and exits. PAIGE *closes the door and turns.*

PAIGE: All right. Here it is.

HELEN: Yes.

PAIGE: Are you ready?

HELEN: Let's do this.

She starts to get undressed.

PAIGE: Shall I . . . get the lights?

HELEN: Yes, please.

In the dark we can only see the vial of sperm, which glows gently as it moves around.

Okay. Should I lie down? We have to hurry.

She takes the vial from PAIGE *and warms it in her hands.*

PAIGE: But you need to get undressed.

HELEN: Right! Maybe I can hold it with my elbow.

She elbows PAIGE *in the head.*

PAIGE: Ow!

HELEN: Sorry! Ah, here, you take it. Don't drop it.

PAIGE: I won't.

HELEN *is struggling.*

HELEN: Stupid belt.

PAIGE: Maybe we put that sexy music back on?

HELEN: We don't have much time. We can't let it get cold.

PAIGE: It needs to stay room temperature. Here, I am keeping it against my skin until you are ready. Relax.

HELEN: I'm relaxed. This is me relaxed. They say to elevate your legs . . . so . . . ah. There. Okay, I'm ready. Go ahead and put it in.

PAIGE: You know the chances of conceiving are better if we actually make love?

HELEN: I don't know if I can . . . on demand like this, I—

PAIGE: Come here. You hold it. Against you.

HELEN: Okay, you're going to get undressed too.

PAIGE: Yes. Come here. Trust this. Trust us.

We hear the sounds of them moving in the dark as they begin to make love.

HELEN: Okay. Oh. Wow. That's . . . oh, babe, that's . . . Yeah.

SCENE 10: NEEDS TO BE A PLUS

The condo some weeks later. Softer light as HELEN *speaks to the audience.*

HELEN: I never thought I'd be able to have children of my own, so I perfected the role of Super Aunt. I come from a big family and so, when we get together, I spend all my time with the kids. You want to go catch frogs in the pond? I'm your girl. Epic camping trips, truly inspiring water balloon fights, and then later heart-to-heart conversations. I'm there.

And now I have my students as well. You know what I find? If you just show up for them every single day and give it everything you've got—they do too. The classroom becomes like . . . like total possibility outside of space and time—it's incredible! You turn around and that awkward teen who was too shy to speak up in class is running for political office. You read the newspaper and a young man you helped to conquer the comma splice has won an award for his novel.

It's like being a parent. You see these kids struggle and overcome obstacles. You laugh together, you love them, and then they go out into the world and they . . . leave.

Beat.

Which is amazing, you know. To see them out there in the world carving their own paths. Sometimes they send a little note or a thank you.

I think I could be a good . . . mom. A good mother. Doesn't the word sound beautiful and terrifying if you apply it to yourself?

The sounds fade into the music for a few moments. When the lights come back up, HELEN *is in the washroom. She has a pregnancy test in her hand.*

Paige? I am doing the test . . . come here!

Lights come up to normal as PAIGE *comes running in.*

PAIGE: You're doing it now? Are you sure it's been enough time?

HELEN: More than enough.

They lean over the test strip together.

PAIGE: I see something coming there . . . Is that—

HELEN: That's a line. It needs to be a plus.

A pause.

PAIGE: It takes some time. There, do I see a second line starting?

HELEN *lets out her breath.*

HELEN: No.

PAIGE: Do we need to wait, or . . . ?

HELEN: No. That's a negative.

PAIGE: Ah.

Beat. She gathers HELEN *to her.*

Ma belle. It's all right.

HELEN: Is it?

PAIGE: It will be.

Lights fade.

SCENE II: HOW'S DOHA?

HELEN *is lit by a computer screen, multi-tasking in semi-darkness. The distinctive sound of a computer-to-computer call as she dials* TRENT. *He answers and is lit up in the blue glow of a screen.*

TRENT: Well hey, stranger.

HELEN: Hi, Trent. How are things? How's Doha.

TRENT: Sandy . . . hot. How's Canada?

HELEN: Snowy . . . cold. Gotta love summer in our home and native land.

TRENT: We killed the small talk in record time. Still mad at me?

HELEN: I wasn't mad.

TRENT: Come on.

A pause.

So, ya knocked up, yet?

HELEN: No.

TRENT: Oh, I figured you were calling to tell me the good news.

HELEN: No, we're . . . still looking.

TRENT: I can help. The baby maker is located right where your two legs meet. Directly in front of your ass.

HELEN: For a donor. We thought we had someone. We tried one time but then he . . . well, he started coming around all the time. He wanted to stay with us . . .

TRENT: Like, live with you . . . ?

HELEN: For a bit. He was in between places and he needed to stay. Paige got freaked out . . . anyway, it's been rugged.

TRENT: Time to just take advantage of modern conveniences and get thee to a sperm bank.

HELEN: But is it fair for a child to grow up never knowing who their biological father is?

TRENT: I don't know. You could ask about three quarters of the kids I grew up with. In fact, ask me. My mom still looks at the milkman with dewy eyes.

HELEN: I'm serious, Trent.

TRENT: Aren't there some donors who agree to be contacted?

HELEN: All the sperm banks in Canada are anonymous. One offers an "open ID" clause, which states that when the child turns a certain age they can request contact info. But even then, the donor can change his mind. What if we have a boy, and he turns twelve and says, "I'll never know my father. This is all your fault. I hate you!"

TRENT: News flash: all kids say "I hate you" to their parents at some point. It's a rite of passage. And all that depriving him of a father crap . . . you can't be hoisting that aboard? Do you know many kids the world over are lucky enough to have even one loving parent committed to their well-being?

HELEN: I know. I agree with you. It's Paige. Anonymous sperm donation is out of the question. So is adoption. You know she was adopted, and she has these very strong feelings about biology and attachment, and I have to respect them.

TRENT: That sounds like the more compelling argument of the two. "Happy wife equals happy life." And that's why I couldn't help you two out, by the way.

HELEN: How do you mean?

TRENT: I wasn't being all precious with my jizz. It's my girl. She wanted . . . we were trying to having kids and . . .

HELEN: You mean right when I asked you . . . ? I see. But you always said you're never going to be tied down with kids.

TRENT: In undergrad? You said the same thing.

HELEN: True.

TRENT: Heading for forty . . . you get to thinking that a few ties might be what tethers you to the earth. And Tamara—she has always wanted kids. They are just drawn to her; it's kind of magical. I mean, you love someone . . . they change your mind, don't they? But she isn't able to carry a baby. We had the tests and all.

HELEN: I'm so sorry.

TRENT: When you asked me . . . we just got the tests back. How am I supposed to tell her that I'll be fathering a child after all, but not ours?

HELEN: I didn't even think—

TRENT: We weren't ready to talk about it—

HELEN: Here I was imagining you were the asshole . . . and it was actually me.

TRENT: If you look back through history, you'll find that's usually the case.

HELEN: Oh, Trent, I am so sorry. Will you think about adopting, or . . .

TRENT: We aren't sure yet. Got to let that sink in first.

HELEN: Damn. Trent, I'm sorry.

TRENT: Thanks.

Pause.

So you two know what you're gonna do?

HELEN: I don't know. It just seems that Paige is putting so many conditions on us that we'll never be able to get pregnant.

TRENT: You want advice?

HELEN: Whatcha got?

TRENT: Woman loves you, yes? You feel totally, wholly loved with no conditions and no BS.

HELEN: Yeah. I do.

TRENT: Stick with her, then. She's got to have her reasons for doing what she'd doing. If you find that with someone, don't give it up. It's the only glimmer of beauty in this smashed-up, messed-up life we lead.

HELEN: Trent?

TRENT: Mm?

HELEN: I've missed you.

TRENT: See? You were mad at me.

HELEN: Okay, a bit. Thanks for listening.

TRENT: Any time. That is, any time given the Calgary–Doha time difference.

Lights fade.

SCENE 12: MISSIONARY MAN

A man in an ill-fitting suit jacket sits across from them. He has a Bible tucked under his right arm.

MISSIONARY: When I saw your words, I knew I had to make the trip into the city.

HELEN: We really appreciate that you've taken the time to come all way here to meet with us.

MISSIONARY: It was nothing. Jesus took the wheel and I had the favoured wind of our saviour at my back.

HELEN: Oh . . . kay. Well, you did read our profile, right? You know that we're married.

PAIGE: To each other?

MISSIONARY: Yes, and that is why I came all the way here today. I want to help you. Join hands with me now, and pray.

He reaches out, but they do not reach back.

HELEN: You want to help us?

MISSIONARY: I want to help you get back on the road to righteousness.

HELEN: Perhaps we have some sort of misunderstanding. You mean, you didn't come here to help us have a baby?

MISSIONARY: To help you make a child that will be born into the scalding flames of hellfire? I am afraid not.

PAIGE: *Ç'est nul.*

HELEN: Keep your temper, Paige.

PAIGE: I'm trying.

MISSIONARY: What we need to do is pray. We can pray the gay away today!

HELEN: Somehow I'm not tempted. Despite your mad rhyming skills . . .

MISSIONARY: Lying with mankind as with womankind is a foul and mortal sin.

HELEN: We're actually going to great lengths *not* to lay with mankind.

MISSIONARY: Homosexuality of any kind is an abomination in the eyes of the Lord!

HELEN: Most biblical scholars disagree. The passages used to condemn homosexuality are all talking about abusive sex. There's no mention whatsoever of loving gay relationships.

The MISSIONARY *continues to recite passages from Leviticus or about Sodom and Gomorrah.*

MISSIONARY: "As Sodom and Gomorrah, and the cities around them in a similar manner to these . . . "

PAIGE: *Laisse tomber* . . . this guy is *complètement fou.*

HELEN: I am just saying that Jesus himself never said anything about gay people.

MISSIONARY: "Having given themselves over to sexual immorality . . . "

PAIGE: No wonder. He and Pontius Pilate . . .

PAIGE winks.

Allez, let's go.

MISSIONARY: "And gone after *strange flesh*, are set forth as an example—"

HELEN: Wait a minute, are you saying Jesus was gay?

PAIGE: I don't want to out a brother. But he might have been, as you say, "on the down low."

MISSIONARY: "To spend all of eternity suffering the vengeance of eternal fire!"

HELEN turns to him.

HELEN: Considering your views on the matter, would getting some sperm be completely out of the question?

MISSIONARY: Will you accept Jesus Christ as your personal saviour and cease living in mortal sin?

HELEN: Still a no for me. Paige?

PAIGE: Pass.

MISSIONARY: Then . . . NO SPERM FOR YOU, OH SPAWN OF SATAN!

HELEN: Okay, thanks for your time all the same.

PAIGE: Are we scraping the bottom of the barrel yet?

HELEN: I thought it went well. All things considered.

Lights fade.

SCENE 13: TWELVE-STEP PROGRAM

A man in work clothes and baseball hat chats with HELEN *and* PAIGE.

LOUIE: I've done about any job you can name. Logging, mining, construction. And none of it is as important as being a good parent. We have five wonderful kids. Two girls and three boys. They are the light and joy of my life.

HELEN: It shows.

LOUIE: I'd keep on having them, too. But my wife says five is enough. And I'm not the one who has to bring them into the world, after all, so she's the boss.

PAIGE: So we are clear: You don't want to be a full-time parent?

HELEN: We've met a couple of guys who would really rather have kids of their own.

LOUIE: No, got my hands full already.

HELEN: But you'd be open to the child knowing that you are his or her biological father? Maybe meet them at some point in the future?

LOUIE: Delighted. We'll bring the two families together. We'll have giant backyard barbecues. Standing invitation for you and the tykes.

HELEN: If you don't mind me asking, what made you think about being a donor?

LOUIE: Out of everything I have accomplished, if I look back over my life . . . nothing compares to the moment when, after half an hour of rocking and pats on the back, I get a really good, satisfied burp out of one of my babies . . . you know?

PAIGE: I can imagine.

LOUIE: I started thinking about all the people out there who might never get a chance to be parents. Just because they are lacking this one little ingredient that I happen to produce every single day.

PAIGE: And your wife doesn't mind.

LOUIE: *Au contraire.* When I told her about you, she said: "Louie, you go help these nice girls start a family. It's your responsibility as a father and a citizen."

HELEN: Wow. She sounds amazing.

LOUIE: She is. I know I'm a lucky man.

HELEN: Since you answered our ad, I guess you're okay with the idea of a two-mom family.

LOUIE: To have not one but two moms, who want you so badly that they go to all this trouble to bring you into the world? This baby is gonna have it made in the shade. Besides, love makes a family. Isn't that what they say?

PAIGE: That is what they say.

HELEN: Wow. Where have you been hiding?

LOUIE: Well now, folks haven't been giving you a hard time, have they? I'd hate to hear that.

PAIGE: Only some attempts to save us from the fires of hell.

HELEN: Pamphlets in the mailbox.

PAIGE: Strange letters from the condo association.

HELEN: Nothing we can't handle. It's just that we were starting to think that we'd never find a donor here. And now here you are. And your wife, your entire lovely family. Altruistic, forward-thinking people. Right in the heart of wild rose country.

PAIGE: Is there something else we can tell you? You'll let us know of your decision soon?

LOUIE: Ladies, I've already made up my mind. I'd be honoured to help you start a family, if you'll accept me.

HELEN: Really?

LOUIE: Absolutely.

PAIGE: Wow! Amazing.

> *PAIGE and HELEN grab one another's hand for a moment and squeeze.*

HELEN: So then, I guess there are a few practicalities we'll have to take care of. I hope you won't feel insulted, but would you mind getting an STI test?

LOUIE: Why would I be insulted? You have to protect yourselves. In fact—

He reaches into his pocket.

Here is a clean bill of health. You can keep that copy.

PAIGE: Okay. That's . . . efficient.

HELEN: I don't know how to thank you.

LOUIE: We could go ahead and try right now.

HELEN: What, now?

LOUIE: This here is my inn. I have a couple loose ends to tie up, but this key is for room 110. I'll meet you there in twenty minutes.

HELEN: No, one of us would have to be ovulating.

PAIGE: And we would need a container to collect the sperm—

LOUIE: What do you mean, collect?

PAIGE: A sterile container into which you . . .

PAIGE motions.

LOUIE: No, that's impossible. I can't do it that way.

HELEN: Our profile says AI: Artificial Insemination.

LOUIE: No, no, no. You have to read up on it. Your chances of getting pregnant are much higher if you have sex.

PAIGE: Your chances are higher of conceiving if you have an orgasm—but that's a different matter entirely.

LOUIE: Orgasm. Did you just say . . . Ohhhkay. Listen. You have to let me . . . I'm sorry, I can only help you out if we do this the old-fashioned way.

HELEN: Wait a minute. Are you saying you won't help us if we don't have sex with you?

LOUIE: Ladies, ladies, don't think of it that way.

PAIGE: *Mais non, ç'est dégoûtant!*

LOUIE: I just want to help you.

HELEN: And you're sitting here talking about your kids and your wife . . . Does your wife even know you're here?

LOUIE: Listen, my wife—

HELEN: Does she?

LOUIE: No, I—my wife—

He drops his head into his hands.

My wife is going to leave me!

PAIGE: I wonder why.

HELEN: Oh, you should be ashamed of yourself!

LOUIE: I *am*—I just can't stop. I can't help myself. I'm in a twelve-step program.

HELEN: For what? Assholes?

LOUIE: Sex addicts. The first step was admitting to myself that I was powerless over my addiction. My name is Louie, and I am a sex addict. I've had to own up to all my mistakes. I'm making progress.

PAIGE: This is progress? You lured us here to see if one of us would sleep with you.

LOUIE: I was hoping for both. Again, I'm sorry that I misled you. That was wrong. But that's not really me, you see? It's the addiction talking. And I didn't even think about how this would feel from your point of view. To get your hopes up and then have them dashed by some jerk only out for his own self-serving agenda.

HELEN: It's not great.

PAIGE: No, it's not.

LOUIE: I am so sorry. See that? That's step number nine: where possible make amends. I've got them all committed to memory. The truth is, this whole thing has just torn my life apart. I used to be someone in this town. But now it's all I can do just to get through the day.

PAIGE: Okay. We're done here.

LOUIE: I can't focus on my work. The inn's in receivership. Soon I won't even have a place to sleep because my wife won't let me come back to the house anymore. But that's no excuse for me to go and haul you into the mess that I call a life. It would mean something to me if you would just accept my apology.

PAIGE: We accept. Goodbye.

HELEN: All right, that's decent.

LOUIE: I mean, you have hopes and dreams just like anyone else.

He throws his arms around HELEN.

I need help.

HELEN *thumps him gently, awkwardly on the back.*

HELEN: You've taken the first step—

LOUIE: Yes, help. That's what I need.

HELEN: Okay that's enough. Paige?

PAIGE *peels him off gently but firmly and frog marches him over to the door.*

PAIGE: You, my friend, are barking up the wrong tree.

LOUIE: I know. I'm sorry. Really nice tree all the same.

HELEN: Don't call us. We definitely won't call you.

Blackout.

SCENE 14: WE'VE BEEN STOOD UP

PAIGE: Okay, next.

Lights change. During this next section, two men play each male role with their backs to the audience, sitting in alternating chairs. The women watch, almost as if it were a tennis match.

MAN: I would have no problem whatsoever being your donor.

HELEN: Really?

MAN: No problem at all. Provided you raise the child a strict vegetarian.

He switches hats.

As long as you promise to send the child to private school.

Switch.

Public school.

Switch.

I will help you have a child as long as you promise to home school him.

Switch.

On one condition: if the child is a boy he must be circumcised.

Switch.

The foreskin must remain intact!

Switch.

Vaccinations are a government conspiracy!

Switch.

The child must be vaccinated, of course . . .

Switch.

As long as he can go into the family business: taxidermy!

Switch.

It would be nice if the child shared my love of silent film.

Switch.

I would of course want to teach him to master the art of bare-knuckle boxing. Go ahead, hit me.

Switch.

I can help you as long as you raise the child as an Orthodox Jew.

Switch.

In accordance with the tenants of the prophet Muhammad.

Switch.

A Catholic.

Switch.

A Protestant!

He starts to take a swing at the Catholic.

A dyed-in-the-wool Liberal.

A staunch Conservative.

A card-carrying member of the Wild Rose Party.

A Rastafarian, man. Peace.

As long as you raise them to be a fan of the greatest hockey team in the history of the sport: the Edmonton Oilers.

The Calgary Flames!

Oilers!

Flames! I'll kill you, man.

Bring it!!

As long as you sign this document saying that, in the event of your sudden and untimely death, the children should go to me.

Switch.

This time the lights come up and there is no one there. The women are waiting.

HELEN: What's he driving?

PAIGE: Blue sedan.

They look up and down the street. A pause.

HELEN: Do you have the container?

PAIGE: Here it is!

Pause.

HELEN: What time is it?

PAIGE: Nearly one. He's late.

HELEN: Very. Did you text or—

PAIGE: I did. He's not answering.

Pause.

HELEN: Are you sure we gave him the—

PAIGE: I'm sure.

Pause.

Ma belle . . . I don't think he is coming.

HELEN: So it appears. Must have changed his mind.

PAIGE: We've been stood up.

HELEN: A new low.

HELEN sighs.

That's it. End of the list. We don't have any other prospects. You heard the fertility doctor: "Your eggs aren't getting any younger."

PAIGE: To hear her, we should have started trying when we were teenagers.

HELEN: Listen, Paige. I know how you feel about the sperm bank—

PAIGE: You don't know how I feel or you would not ask.

HELEN: For something this important, don't you think you could put your principles aside?

PAIGE: This is deeper than a principle. Can't you understand?

HELEN: I keep doing all the asking, putting myself out there, and meanwhile you—

PAIGE: I can't talk to people like you can—the language—

HELEN: You always blame that—

PAIGE: But it *is* harder.

HELEN: For something like this, though? You haven't even asked one person and you act like it doesn't matter.

PAIGE: Of course it matters, Helen.

HELEN: That's not fair. You're the one who started this.

PAIGE: We started it together.

HELEN: You made me want to be a mother. And now . . . I can't stop thinking about it. I mean, what if we can't . . . do this?

PAIGE: Yes, what if?

HELEN: And it's just us. No little feet. No kissing boo-boos.

PAIGE: I lived with the question of where I came from my whole life. There are so many things I want to pass on to a child . . . but not that.

HELEN: What if that's the only way?

PAIGE: Then we might not have children.

HELEN: I never let myself want anything like this before and now . . . I do. It's like I found this huge hole that I didn't know was in my heart. And when you asked me if I wanted to have a baby with you,

I just let myself admit that YES, YES, I want that. I've always wanted little arms around my neck, and art on the fridge, and cheering from the sidelines. Now you're giving up?

PAIGE: I want it, too. But not at any cost.

HELEN: Cost? What cost?

PAIGE: Us, maybe.

HELEN: Don't say that.

PAIGE: You're not listening to me.

HELEN: I am!

PAIGE: *Comme si tu es allé quelque part. [It's like you've gone off somewhere.]* Not even in the room.

HELEN: I'm right here. What is it, Paige?

PAIGE: That hole in your heart. When did I stop being enough to fill it?

HELEN: That's not what I said.

PAIGE: You say "just" us. Aren't we enough?

HELEN: I . . . I don't know.

PAIGE: If you and I are suddenly not enough . . . then we have no base to build anything on.

HELEN: You. You made me want this. And now I see them, these children we don't yet have. Sitting at this counter you've built eating a bowl of Cheerios—it's like they're here, but they're not. I mean, what are we tearing the place apart for anyway? Why are you making a nursery if . . . if . . .

HELEN gets her jacket, heads for the door.

PAIGE: Where are you going?

HELEN: *Je dois sortir d'ici. [I have to get out of here.]*

PAIGE: Don't do this.

HELEN: I just need . . . I need to think.

PAIGE: Don't go out that door, Helen.

She leaves. PAIGE thinks about going after her but changes her mind.

SCENE 15: NOT A SLAB

PAIGE is working on the renovations. Concrete and drywall dust cover the surfaces and her.

KYLE enters with samples of different kinds of granite.

PAIGE: Thanks for fitting us in. I know you have a backlog right now.

KYLE: Not a problem. You had my back on that duplex job last month. I'll give you the tradesman's rate on the granite itself. Basically at cost.

PAIGE: Very kind.

KYLE: And I imagine you'll want to be here when we drop it in—

PAIGE: For certain.

KYLE: So, if we have you, I can get away with hiring one other guy. Keep the labour costs down for you. Maybe you can spring for the high-end stuff.

PAIGE: Thank you, Kyle. I really appreciate it.

He pulls out some pieces of stone and sets them on the half-finished countertop.

KYLE: Check out this. Bianco Romano in a grey palate. Pretty classic and pairs well with walnut or oak cabinets. If you want to go stainless steel, on the other hand, this would work. You really have to see the stone in place, I find.

He looks around at the renovations.

So you're taking out this wall?

PAIGE: Yes, my idea is to reclaim part of the kitchen to make a second bedroom. It will be smaller, but I hope still functional.

KYLE: So an island here with a range hood? Recessed lighting . . . nice. The right materials can really make it pop. You settled on granite? For resale value it's a no-brainer, but quartz is a good plan B if you are worried about wear and tear and so on. So which way are you leaning?

PAIGE: Yes, that sounds very good.

KYLE: Which one?

PAIGE: Sorry?

KYLE: That was an either-or question.

PAIGE: Of course, of course, I—

KYLE checks phone.

KYLE: Shit. I am supposed to be across town already. Mrs. Honeywell will have my head on a platter. I'll leave these with you and just give me a shout when you decide.

PAIGE: Wait, Kyle. I have something to ask you.

KYLE: Shoot.

PAIGE: Oh, *merde.* You see I—we—

KYLE: What's up? You feeling okay?

PAIGE: No, actually . . .

KYLE: Eat something off? I had food poisoning last month and it kicked my ass.

PAIGE: This is not . . . not related to countertops.

Pause.

This is . . . difficult for me. The language.

KYLE: Don't sweat it. Your English is better than mine.

PAIGE: You just seem to be a . . . a really good person. We don't know each other well—

KYLE: Well enough.

PAIGE: But what I see of you, I like.

He had been packing up his tools, but he pauses now and listens carefully.

KYLE: Paige, listen.

PAIGE: Okay, now I must just go for it, or I lose my nerve. I like your candour. The way you carry yourself—this is going to come into the blue, as you say—

KYLE: Out of.

PAIGE: Sorry?

KYLE: The expression is "out of the blue," but it doesn't matter. Look, um—

PAIGE: My wife and I have been having a problem and I have to do something—before one of us goes insane.

KYLE: I think I know what you want . . .

He walks toward her.

PAIGE: You do?

KYLE: It's pretty evident that your mind has been on something else since I got here. I wish I could say this was the first time it's happened.

PAIGE: Really? Others have asked you—

KYLE: But I didn't expect it from your corner. And, frankly, it's not even flattering, it's insulting.

PAIGE: The last thing I want is to insult you. I—

KYLE: You think that I'm a slab of stone that can be ordered up and delivered?

PAIGE: NO, not at all! I mean, I am not asking you to engage in sex, all I want is for you to ejaculate into—

KYLE: Okay, I got to stop you there—

PAIGE: *Merde.*

KYLE: You know me, I am not a judgmental person. You and your girl get your freak on, but leave me out of it.

PAIGE: Oh, I mess this up terribly. *Je me suis désolé* . . . I never—

Beat.

Listen, Kyle. I am sorry. Can we just forget this conversation ever happened?

He nods.

KYLE: Of course, no harm, no foul.

They shake hands.

He exits. When she hears the outside door close, PAIGE *picks up some boards and hurls them aside in frustration.*

SCENE 16: RASH DECISIONS

A corner dive bar. HELEN and EVAN are doing shots. The empty soldiers are lined up in front of them.

EVAN: So then I told him, flat out, "Tim, you have to treat me like an equal partner in this relationship." I really spoke my mind—it felt great.

HELEN: Good for you.

EVAN: I'm not sure what sunk in. He was watching *MasterChef* at the same time. I need another round.

HELEN: Me too.

EVAN: Shouldn't you take it easy?

HELEN: No. No prospects at the moment. Paige and I had a bit of a—you know this whole thing really messes with your emotions.

EVAN: Tell me about it. Every time I bring up the subject of children with Tim, I can count on a scene. Men!

HELEN: You think men are difficult? Try dealing with a woman.

Her phone buzzes; she turns it off.

EVAN: I'll drink to that.

HELEN: And it's pretty ridiculous, because if everyone would behave, we could all have what we wanted. For what it's worth, I'm really sorry it didn't work out.

EVAN: Probably for the best. At least you were open and clear about what you wanted from the beginning. Not everyone is.

HELEN: Oh. Have you done this before?

EVAN: I tried. There was this girl who promised that if I helped her make a baby I could— No, you called me up to come cheer you up—

HELEN: That's okay, I want to hear it.

EVAN: I helped her set up—she was living on the edge a bit, and you know you can't if you are pregnant.

HELEN: Of course not.

EVAN: So we got her an apartment and I went to prenatal with her . . . I was there when the baby was born—I caught her—and then the mother, she—

HELEN: No . . .

EVAN: Broke contact.

HELEN: But isn't there something you can do, I mean . . .

He shakes his head.

EVAN: We didn't have a formal agreement, and even if we did . . .

HELEN: Evan, I think you'd be a great dad.

EVAN: Thanks. I'm glad you called me. Surprised, but glad.

HELEN: Me too. Have you always known that you wanted children?

EVAN: Always. My biggest fear when I realized that I was attracted to men was that I would never be able to have a family. So I resisted it for a long time. I used to look around at all my female friends . . . wonder if it might be better to stick it out with one of them. Try to make it work.

HELEN: But that's no way to live.

EVAN: In the end, I couldn't do it. But who knows . . . I know guys who did that. Got married, had children . . . came out later in life. And now they have all this . . . a whole generation after them . . . and they found love, too. And here I am. Stuck.

HELEN: Tim seems to have made up his mind.

EVAN: The thing is, I just can't stop picturing what our lives would be like if we could have a child. Tim is so brilliant and funny. And—you couldn't see it the other night—he really is gentle and kind. He would have so much to give as a parent.

HELEN: Not if he doesn't want it.

EVAN: I know, so I have to let it go. But that's enough Tim and Evan talk. It's making me depressed. How about you? Did you always know you wanted to be a mother?

HELEN: I never thought I could, but when Paige asked me . . . something shifted inside me. Like a clicking into place. And now I can't turn it back.

EVAN: You're so lucky.

HELEN: I don't feel lucky. I feel lost.

EVAN: Ironic, isn't it? I mean, here we sit. The egg and the sperm. All the necessary ingredients to produce a baby . . . but it just won't work.

HELEN: We could just go do this. We could go make a baby and let the chips fall where they may.

EVAN: You mean, don't tell our partners? Go behind their backs? Oh, Tim would be furious.

HELEN: Once the baby comes all warm and pink and real they'll sort themselves out.

EVAN: You don't mean that we—you and I?

HELEN: No. No! We just need a sterile container of some kind.

There are shot glasses lined up in front of them. HELEN *points to one.*

EVAN: But isn't it irresponsible to begin a life . . . a brand-new life, in this haphazard way?

HELEN: I myself am the product of a bottle of great white, a rainy night, and a poorly made decision. My folks didn't have a clue, didn't really love each other. They made a mistake and, sure, it uprooted their lives, but that mistake is me. And they love me. Here I am.

EVAN: I am finding your argument strangely compelling.

HELEN: Why should we hold ourselves to a higher standard?

EVAN: Or maybe it's the gin.

HELEN: God forbid we let the straight people corner the market on rash decisions.

EVAN *tucks a shot glass into his coat pocket. They exit, somewhat tipsily.*

SCENE 17: VERY FIRST MOMENT

Later that evening. We hear rain on the roof. HELEN *comes in, quite tipsy.*

PAIGE: Where have you been?

HELEN: Listen, Paige. There is something I need to tell you. Really important.

HELEN *trips trying to get her boots off.* PAIGE *steadies her.*

PAIGE: I left you five messages. I was this close to filing a missing person's report.

HELEN: You're beautiful. You're a really beautiful woman.

PAIGE: You've been drinking.

HELEN: I need to tell you—us, all of this: a total accident. Crossing of countries. Uprooting of lives. But for a chance meeting. A cup of coffee spilled. A delayed flight.

PAIGE: You're drunk.

HELEN: No, I missed it on purpose. I never told you that.

PAIGE: Let's get this coat off of you.

HELEN: Just so I could keep talking to you. It was that first moment you put your hand on my arm. All of a sudden I felt like everything that was happening to me was happening for a reason. And this voice, this voice inside telling me not to let you go away from me. Not to lose you.

PAIGE: You missed your flight on purpose?

HELEN: I could see the boarding call on the screen right behind you. Paige, what if this were the first moment? What if we were starting all over again, like the big bang or . . . no, what if we were just little specks of life floating in the ocean?

PAIGE: You need water. Or a cup of tea.

HELEN: Would your speck love my speck, no matter what? Answer me, I need to know.

PAIGE: If I had the smallest idea what you were talking about—

HELEN: Paige, what would you say if I were just suddenly, magically pregnant? Right now. Wouldn't it solve everything? It would be what we wanted, right?

PAIGE pulls away from her.

PAIGE: What did you do?

HELEN: What if it didn't matter how it happened. What if this were the very first moment we met? What if we were starting over again, right now?

PAIGE: You mean, what if you went out and got pregnant behind my back?

HELEN: Would you turn me away?

PAIGE: What did you do, Helen?

HELEN: No, no. I didn't. I wanted to, but I couldn't. What I am trying to say is . . . Plato says, in the *Symposium* . . . we spend our whole lives searching for our other half. You *are* enough, even if it ends up being just us. I found you. You're mine.

PAIGE holds her for a moment.

PAIGE: *Allez, ma belle.* Let's go to bed. You will feel this tomorrow.

Blackout.

SCENE 18: LAST KIND STRANGER

PAIGE: We kept on looking for another year.

HELEN: In total, it was closer to two. We went back to Evan to see if we might work something out . . . but by then his partner had done a total one-eighty.

PAIGE: They found a surrogate. They're going to have a child of their own.

HELEN: We sifted through every email. Followed every possible lead.

PAIGE: We knew he had to be out there somewhere. Our "Mr. Right." A man who wanted only to help. To be part of a child's life—and ours.

HELEN: The last kind stranger in the modern world and, when we finally found him, we nearly choked.

PAIGE: We nearly scared him away.

The lights reveal a man in partial silhouette. PAIGE and HELEN fire questions at him. They may begin to pace, interrogation-style, at some point. He is taken aback at first.

HELEN: We'll need to see recent STI tests.

PAIGE: And fertility tests, too.

HELEN: We need your blood type. Also, what is your motivation for being a donor? Are you sure you don't want to be a parent yourself?

PAIGE: We want to be clear that you won't have any parental rights whatsoever.

HELEN: That's right. We have a contract.

PAIGE: You won't ask to raise them in any certain way?

HELEN: Or have us sign any quasi-legal documents about our future impending deaths?

PAIGE: You don't want to live with us?

KIND STRANGER: Ah, no.

PAIGE: Or propose an impromptu threesome?

He clears his throat.

KIND STRANGER: No, I didn't have anything like that in mind.

PAIGE: *Je suis désolé.* I am sorry. You see, we've met with a lot of different men.

HELEN: And they all seem to want something from us . . . other than what we propose.

PAIGE: It's been quite hard.

KIND STRANGER: I can imagine.

PAIGE: Yes, asking a stranger or someone you've just met for this favour . . . So intimate.

KIND STRANGER: Yes. It requires trust and good faith . . .

HELEN: Yes.

KIND STRANGER: Two things that are, sadly, in short supply these days.

HELEN: Exactly!

PAIGE: Can we just ask you why? Why would you want to help us?

A spotlight comes up on the KIND STRANGER. *He seems to be lifted up on a pedestal, superhero-like.*

KIND STRANGER: It's pretty simple. We've only known each other a short while, but you seem like you'd be great parents.

PAIGE: *Merci.*

HELEN: Thanks.

KIND STRANGER: Let's just say that I have been . . . on the receiving end of a pretty huge favour myself, and I vowed that if I ever got the chance . . . I would pay it forward.

HELEN: Really?

KIND STRANGER: Sure, I would like to get to know the child or children if this works out. But no strings attached. If you manage to conceive a child, I would be really happy for you. This seems like my chance to create something good in the world . . . and I just don't want to miss out.

We begin to hear a choir of angels . . . but it's cut short.

When the lights come back up on HELEN*, she is pregnant.*

HELEN: And we were tempted to make this man, this kind man who helped us get pregnant—

PAIGE *steps into the light—she is also pregnant.*

PAIGE: Both of us, one right after the other—

HELEN: We would have been happy at the prospect of one baby.

PAIGE: But with two, we are ecstatic!

HELEN: And so it was tempting to turn him into a kind of superhero. But that wouldn't be right either.

PAIGE: We have to let him be—be what he is. Someone who helped us in a way that we will never, ever be able to fully thank him for.

HELEN: And let him know . . . this baby.

PAIGE: And this one. And see what happens.

They hold hands.

People thought we were insane.

HELEN: Two pregnant women under one roof. The hormones!

PAIGE: Who will run to get ice cream? And the pickles for on top? Who should tie the shoes?

HELEN: We've come back to our little place near the ocean to have the babies. It might be primordial. Maybe we all want to return to origins when we make our nests.

PAIGE: People do sometimes turn their heads at us in this small town when we walk by holding hands . . . both bellies out in front.

HELEN: Yesterday Paige had some labour pains and we thought . . . this is it! We roared up in front of the hospital and I helped her out, saying, "Come on, sweetie, do the breathing. Do the breathing. I love you. You can do this.

PAIGE: And the poor man on the bench—

HELEN: There's this guy. In a doeskin and hat and he's just gaping at us like he's staring down a couple of Martians, for god's sake. I'm hot and tired and pregnant and I have just had it and so I yell, "HEY, BUDDY, WHAT'S THE MATTER? HAVEN'T YOU EVER SEEN A COUPLE OF PREGNANT LESBIANS BEFORE??" And he just takes off his hat and shakes his head and says, "Ma'am, I'm really sorry, I'm afraid I have not."

PAIGE: He's a really nice man. The labour pains stopped.

HELEN: It was Braxton Hicks.

PAIGE: False alarm.

HELEN: And we ended up having coffee with him. Told him our whole story.

PAIGE: He's promised to visit when the babies are born.

HELEN: It goes to show you, they're out there after all—the kind strangers. You just have to look.

As the lights fade, we hear the sounds of a delivery room. Doctors and nurses offer encouragement. We hear PAIGE *and* HELEN *during labour and encouraging one another. A building chorus of exclamations from everyone until we hear the distinctive first cry of a newborn baby . . . and then a second one. The newborns' cries mix with joyous exclamations.*

The end.

ACKNOWLEDGEMENTS

Many thanks to everyone at Lunchbox Theatre, DMV Theatre, Neptune Theatre, and Ruby Slippers Theatre for helping this play find its first audiences. Thank you to everyone at the Playwrights Guild of Canada, the Playwrights Atlantic Resource Centre, and Playwrights Canada Press for your work on behalf of Canadian playwrights. Thank you to Miranda Botto, Director of Marketing and Communications for Lunchbox Theatre, for help obtaining the rights for the cover image. Thank you to every actor who has lent your chops to the play, and to Dianne Richards for her careful editing eyes.

Natalie Meisner is a widely produced author of stage plays and an award-winning multi-genre author. Her play *Boom Baby* (about the lives of workers in the Alberta oil patch) won both the Canadian National Playwriting Competition and the Alberta Playwriting Competition. *Double Pregnant: Two Lesbians Make a Family* topped non-fiction bestseller lists and was a finalist in the Atlantic Book Awards. Her first children's book, *My Mommy, My Mama, My Brother & Me*, is available from Nimbus Publishing. Other books include *Baddie One Shoe*, a collection of poetic odes to renegades of the past and present, and *Legislating Love: The Everett Klippert Story*, a play about the last person in Canada to be jailed for homosexuality. Meisner is a wife and mom to two great boys and a professor in the Department of English at Mount Royal University, where she works in the areas of creative writing, drama, and gender/sexuality studies.

First edition: April 2020
Printed and bound in Canada by Rapido Books, Montreal

Cover artwork provided on behalf of Lunchbox Theatre from the world premiere of *Speed Dating for Sperm Donors* during their 2014/2015 season.
Author photo © D. Mounsef

PLAYWRIGHTS CANADA PRESS

202-269 Richmond St. W.
Toronto, ON
M5V 1X1

416.703.0013
info@playwrightscanada.com
www.playwrightscanada.com
@playcanpress